Loneliness
Therapy

MW00416325

Loneliness Therapy

written by
Daniel Grippo

illustrated by
R.W. Alley

ONE
CARING
PLACE

Abbey Press

Text © 2002 by Daniel Grippo
Illustrations © 2002 by St. Meinrad Archabbey
Published by One Caring Place
Abbey Press
St. Meinrad, Indiana 47577

All rights reserved.
No part of this book may be used or reproduced in any manner
without written permission of the publisher, except in the case of
brief quotations embodied in critical articles and reviews.

Library of Congress Catalog Number
2002100908

ISBN 0-87029-363-X

Printed in the United States of America

Foreword

Are you lonely? If so, you're definitely not alone!

Loneliness is widespread in contemporary society. Seems the faster we go, and the more high-tech our ways of staying connected become, the more common it becomes to feel alone and disconnected.

Loneliness tells us that something's out of balance, that something is missing in our lives. Maybe that "something" is a very dear loved one who has died. Other times, a serious illness might throw life out of balance and leave us feeling all alone. Loneliness is extra tough when it comes mixed with grief or illness.

Whether your loneliness is the result of a death or illness, or any of life's other transitions, *Loneliness Therapy* can help. It explores a variety of experiences—some passing, others more chronic—that can bring about loneliness, and offers gentle, practical suggestions that point the way toward relief.

The good news is, there *is* life beyond loneliness. You can move beyond isolation to a feeling—and an experience—of connectedness, of belonging. This little book, with its wise elfin characters, is designed to help you find ways of connecting with yourself, with others, with God.

1.

All of us feel lonely from time to time. A bit of loneliness, like a bit of rain, falls on everyone. Usually the skies clear soon enough, but when they don't, it's a sign that we need to look deeper.

2.

Persistent loneliness is a feeling that tells us our lives are incomplete or out of balance in some way. Loneliness isn't the problem—it's the <u>symptom</u> that lets us know there's a problem.

3.

Anything that upsets the balance you have achieved in life can lead to loneliness. Many of life's major transitions can leave you feeling lonely, sometimes for a little while, sometimes for much longer.

4.

When someone you love very much dies, the loneliness you feel can be overwhelming. You may feel abandoned, alone, adrift in uncharted waters.

5.

A serious illness, especially
one that keeps you homebound,
can leave you feeling very lonely.
The pain and fear that come
with illness only heighten
your feelings of isolation.

6.

Where death or illness is concerned, a visit from a friend can do much to lift your spirits. Don't be afraid to ask for a visit—a good friend will leap at the chance to be with you when you need company.

7.

When a relationship ends, or a loved one leaves home, you can't help but experience some loneliness, especially if you're left with an "empty nest." Pursuing a new interest that brings you together with others will help.

8.

It's not at all unusual to feel lonely in a crowd. Remember, it's not the number of people around you that counts, but whether you feel connected to them.

9.

Feeling all alone when others are celebrating is especially hard. Maybe there's someone else who feels the same way and would like to talk. Seek them out!

10.

People are so mobile these days, it's not unusual to feel disconnected from your community. When loved ones move far away, it only heightens the sense of isolation.

11.

Something as simple as striking up a conversation with a neighbor over the fence can be enough to help you begin to feel connected. Or have a garage sale and see who drops by!

YARD
SALE
today

12.

Volunteering is a great way to feel connected to your community and meet new people, while doing something to make the world a better place. Sometimes getting outside yourself for a while is the surest path to feeling better.

13.

If family problems or divisions
leave you feeling lonely or
estranged, extend an olive
branch to help heal the hurt.
Do what you can to bring
loved ones together again.

14.

The holidays are supposed to be a time of warm celebration, but sometimes they can leave you feeling cold and lonely, especially if you've recently lost a loved one.

15.

Anniversaries, birthdays, and other important "milestones" are also very difficult after a loved one's death or departure. Be sure to spend time with a good friend on these difficult days, or use some simple ritual that brings comfort.

16.

Losing a job hits hard on many levels. The sense of isolation can be very powerful. While you're looking for new work, also look for people who understand what you're going through and can be supportive.

17.

Moving to a new town can be exciting. But don't be surprised if it also brings feelings of loneliness for a while. Give yourself time to make new connections.

18.

Starting a new job is supposed to be an adventure. But it can also leave you feeling awkward and out of place for a while, until you get to know your new coworkers. Be patient—you'll feel better soon.

19.

The gold watch at retirement is nice, but it won't replace the camaraderie you had with your coworkers. Use your new-found freedom to find new ways of being active and involved.

20.

Your team's season is over, your community theater show has closed, or the big group project at work is done, and everyone's gone home—now what do you do? It's hard to come down from the "high" that working toward a common goal brings.

21.

Kids feel lonely, too. Being "different" from the other kids, whether that means being extra smart or a little slow, extra big or on the small side, can leave a young person feeling alone and unloved.

22.

Being a different color or speaking a different language—being different in any way—can leave a person of any age feeling shunned. Being shunned is no fun. Fortunately, many people welcome and embrace diversity. Seek them out.

23.

If you're physically challenged, you might feel like there's no one in the world who understands "what it's like." But there <u>are</u> others who understand—don't stop looking until you find them.

24.

Older people aren't always treated with the respect and dignity they deserve. If you find that being old leaves you feeling isolated and undervalued, contact a social service agency or local church to see what programs they have for seniors. You have much to share with a world that is short on wisdom!

25.

Sometimes it's not who you are but something you've done that leaves you feeling all alone. If you do something that drives others away, admit it and ask for forgiveness. Be just as willing to forgive others their shortcomings. Reconciliation overcomes loneliness in a big way.

26.

Like an unwelcome weed in the garden, persistent loneliness has to be pulled out at the roots. Dig for answers to questions such as: When do I feel most lonely? Is there a pattern to my loneliness? What helps the most when I feel lonely?

27.

Loneliness, if unattended, can lead us into compulsive and addictive behaviors. Severe loneliness is such a sharp pain that we need to pay attention to it immediately in order to avoid doing damage to ourselves or to others.

28.

Some things in life can't be changed, but many things can be. Make a list of changes you can begin to make that will help you during the times you feel most lonely.

29.

Try to expand the range of your activities and associations. Take a class, join a club, take up a new sport, spend more time with a faith community. An active life leaves little room for loneliness.

30.

Tired of living alone? Advertise for a roommate or move to a more communal setting. Remember the poet's wisdom: "No man (or woman...or elf!) is an island."

31.

If your loneliness persists despite your best efforts, talk to a professional counselor or spiritual advisor. They can help you find your way through the often tangled web of emotions that surround loneliness.

32.

Sometimes loneliness is accompanied by a feeling of spiritual emptiness. If you feel distant from God, it's hard to feel close to your neighbor.

33.

One way to reconnect with
God is to find a time and place
to pray or meditate, or simply
to sit quietly. Getting in touch
with your inner spirit helps you
reach out to others.

34.

When you feel loneliness
coming over you, remind
yourself that there is always
One who walks by your side.

35.

When you pray or worship, alone or with others, you can invite God to fill the emptiness you feel within. Trust that God will respond to your prayer.

36.

Remember that being alone is not the same as feeling lonely. Sometimes being on your own feels very good. When it feels right and brings you peace, it's called solitude, and it's good for the soul.

37.

Use moments of solitude to quietly reflect on what your loneliness has taught you. Maybe you've realized how much someone has meant to you; maybe you've learned that you need to reach out to others to feel connected and alive.

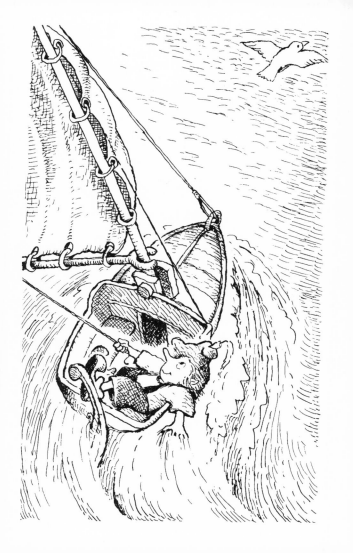

38.

Though loneliness is a painful feeling, the insights that come in its wake are blessings. As you move out of loneliness and into an ever-greater sense of connectedness, cherish those insights—you've earned them!

Daniel Grippo is an editor for the One Caring Place division of Abbey Press, and an editor and publisher for TrueQuest Communications of Chicago. He is the author of *Worry Therapy* (20093) and a variety of other Abbey Press publications. He can be reached at <u>dgrippo@truequest.biz</u>. He would like to dedicate this book to his sister Teri Stanley, in thanks for her many years of friendship.

Illustrator for the Abbey Press Elf-help Books, **R.W. Alley** also illustrates and writes children's books. He lives in Barrington, Rhode Island, with his wife, daughter, and son.

The Story of the Abbey Press Elves

The engaging figures that populate the Abbey Press "elf-help" line of publications and products first appeared in 1987 on the pages of a small self-help book called *Be-good-to-yourself Therapy*. Shaped by the publishing staff's vision and defined in R.W. Alley's inventive illustrations, they lived out author Cherry Hartman's gentle, self-nurturing advice with charm, poignancy, and humor.

Reader response was so enthusiastic that more Elf-help Books were soon under way, a still-growing series that has inspired a line of related gift products.

The especially endearing character featured in the early books—sporting a cap with a mood-changing candle in its peak—has since been joined by a spirited female elf with flowers in her hair.

These two exuberant, sensitive, resourceful, kindhearted, lovable sprites, along with their lively elfin community, reveal what's truly important as they offer messages of joy and wonder, playfulness and co-creation, wholeness and serenity, the miracle of life and the mystery of God's love.

With wisdom and whimsy, these little creatures with long noses demonstrate the elf-help way to a rich and fulfilling life.

Elf-help Books

...adding "a little character" and a lot
of help to self-help reading!

New Baby Therapy	#20140
Teacher Therapy	#20145
Stress Therapy	#20153
Making-sense-out-of-suffering Therapy	#20156
Get Well Therapy	#20157
Anger Therapy	#20127
Caregiver Therapy	#20164
Self-esteem Therapy	#20165
Peace Therapy	#20176
Friendship Therapy	#20174
Christmas Therapy (color edition) $5.95	#20175
Grief Therapy	#20178
Happy Birthday Therapy	#20181
Forgiveness Therapy	#20184
Keep-life-simple Therapy	#20185
Celebrate-your-womanhood Therapy	#20189
Acceptance Therapy (color edition) $5.95	#20182
Acceptance Therapy	#20190
Keeping-up-your-spirits Therapy	#20195

Slow-down Therapy	#20203
One-day-at-a-time Therapy	#20204
Prayer Therapy	#20206
Be-good-to-your-marriage Therapy	#20205
Be-good-to-yourself Therapy (hardcover) $10.95	#20196
Be-good-to-yourself Therapy	#20255

Book price is $4.95 unless otherwise noted.
Available at your favorite giftshop or bookstore—
or directly from One Caring Place, Abbey Press
Publications, St. Meinrad, IN 47577.
Or call 1-800-325-2511.
www.carenotes.com